Crescendo Publishing Presents

Instant Insights on...

RELATIONSHIPS

7 Strategies *for*
Raising Calm, Inspired,
& Successful Children

Dr. Elaine Fogel Schneider, Ph.D.

small guides. BIG IMPACT.

Dear Joan,
You are so spec...
I am so glad you are...
Much joy & Love, Elaine

Instant Insights On...

**7 Strategies for Raising Calm, Inspired &
Successful Children**
By Elaine Fogel Schneider

ISBN: 978-1-944177-47-8 (p)
ISBN: 978-1-944177-48-5 (e)

Crescendo Publishing, LLC
300 Carlsbad Village Drive
Ste. 108A, #443
Carlsbad, California 92008-2999

www.CrescendoPublishing.com
GetPublished@CrescendoPublishing.com

What You'll Learn in this Book

There is much to learn about raising children, especially when you want what's best for them. How do you raise children to be calm, inspired, and successful? The *7 Strategies for Raising Calm, Inspired, and Successful Children* shares strategies and many activities to create new, fun rituals and routines at homes, in schools, or in clinics!

You will learn to bring calm to your children and to improve their learning and overall well-being. Acknowledging busy schedules in everyone's life, each activity is designed to take just a few minutes and can be part of morning hellos in the classroom, simple farewells going out the door to school, ways to connect during television commercial breaks at home, openings to a therapy session, or part of relaxing while looking up at the sky!

You will discover the most recent scientific evidence of why these seven strategies are so beneficial for learning and living successfully. You will learn the calming breath, amazing affirmations, a tender touch, mindfulness moments, loud (and soft) laughter, magical movement and song, and the science of it all.

I couldn't think of any better way to start off a young child's life of productivity and success at home, in the classroom, or anywhere else they go than by learning the strategies you will find under one book cover. Come along and look inside because you get two for the price of one. ... In addition to your child learning and benefitting from these seven strategies, you'll benefit too!

You'll get **Instant Insights** on ...

- Scientific evidence that supports mind-body strategies for improved learning
- Why calm children learn more and have more success
- Strategies that are useful anywhere—home, school, clinics, indoors, or outdoors
- Activities for each strategy that are fun, easy, and quick to administer
- How these strategies benefit the adult offering them in addition to the children learning them

A Gift from the Author

To help you implement the strategies mentioned in this *Instant Insights™* book and get the most value from the content, the author has prepared the following bonus gifts we know you will love:

A FREE app for your iPhone or iPad that will give you all the strokes and information about the benefits of massage for your child:
Baby Massage Basics App for iPhone and iPad

A downloadable list of ten easy strategies for releasing stress that you can carry with you and use each day:
Ten Tension Tamers

A fact sheet of scientific studies that supports the rationale for using breathing, affirmations, touch, mindfulness, laughter, movement and music at home, in classrooms or clinics, for raising calm, inspired, and successful children:
Science Supports Our Intuition

You can get instant access to these complimentary materials here:
http://askdrelaine.com

Dedication

To Memphis and Finley, growing and learning together, you are the best. I love you to the moon and stars and back, and Pop Pop for bringing love and calm into our lives always!

Disclaimer

Any user of these *7 Strategies for Raising Calm, Inspired, and Successful Children* materials, instruction, and presented exercises, advice, and information, assumes their own risk utilizing suggested strategies for self-awareness and for improved physical and emotional health. This book is in no way a substitute for medical and/or professional intervention. Any user of the *7 Strategies for Raising Calm, Inspired, and Successful Children* materials assumes their own risk utilizing these strategies for themselves and/or their children, foster children, adopted children, children attending daycare, preschools, and elementary schools.

If you have any questions about this disclaimer, you may contact info@askdrelaine.com.

Table of Contents

Introduction

"It's not always what you are doing that matters; it is rather how you are being."
-Dr. Elaine Fogel Schneider

If you are like me, what you want for the children in your care, or any child, is always the very best! As the world keeps moving at an enormously fast pace, with modern technology changing in front of our own eyes and events around the world and within our own country affecting our own safety and security, nowhere in time has it been more important for children to be able to find ways to calm themselves, stay focused, learn, and achieve peace within themselves—and with others—to be successful.

As a therapist, trainer, and parent coach for over thirty-five years, I've discovered simple strategies for young children that work to enrich their lives. Being trained in various disciplines (speech, dance/ movement, psychology, touch communication, with specialties in early intervention, special needs, and mental health), my purpose is directed in finding ways to create possibilities for children and families in the home, in the school setting, in clinics, and in the community to reach their full potential.

We live in an era where there are many gadgets that can keep our children's interest and keep them busy, but do they help our children learn about themselves on a personal level? What happens when the child loses at a video game? What happens when a child decides that they want to play with a toy that their classmate or sibling wants too? How do they work things out together? Are they able to take turns, or do they have a giant meltdown?

I've seen three-year-old children come to school who haven't slept through the night. One child I met would never fall asleep until 3:00 a.m. His mother did not know what she could do to entice him to sleep, and he roamed around the house while others slept, or he played on his tablet or left the television set on. He could not really function in his daily activities, and he could not truly regulate his behavior. He did not seek out others and did not acknowledge his feelings. Nurturing touch releases hormones that ease sleep and relaxation. Using nurturing touch may have been a way for this mom to assist her child and help relax him to sleep.

How many of you are having a difficult time falling asleep? How many of you feel out of control yourself, working double jobs, trying to balance jobs and families, or balancing other children while trying to get your own needs met? Does your body ache? Are you burning the candle at both ends and unraveling right in front of the eyes of your own children? What is your model for balance? As a role model, strategies for your own calmness, inspiration, and success are important too.

Researchers show that when you are relaxed you can learn more easily, effecting better academic outcomes. The human brain has a plasticity and can keep learning. Yes, you CAN teach old dogs new tricks! Imagine what you can teach young children, especially when learning takes place when we are calm. Habits are developed early. Bring a child into finding ways to be peaceful, and you will find a child who, when older, has better opportunities to make decisions, enjoy what life offers, and feel more inner peace.

Children are gaining many health benefits by slowing down their minds and being able to connect with others. Scientists are revealing how calmness affects better academic outcomes.

The next seven chapters explore various mind-body strategies for the young child (three to seven years) with three easy, quick, fun activities for each strategy. These strategies can be used seven days of the week. Vary them, combine them, or select one strategy that can be used over and over again.

The seven strategies are in the areas of breathing, affirmations, touch, mindfulness, laughter, movement, and song. Each chapter explains the science behind the benefits. Along with the three fun activities included in each chapter are three Instant Insights too!

For example, breathing facilitates being focused, alert, and relaxed. Being focused leads to success. Use the breathing exercises in the morning, throughout the day, or when an event occurs that is frightening or upsetting. You can incorporate these strategies to become routines and rituals in the home, classroom, or clinic. As you instruct children in these activities, you will benefit too!

Today, our children may be held captive in their apartments or homes as parents are not able to let their children go outside to play, so children may be indulged with tablets or smart phones "to keep them busy and quiet." But is their quiet time really quiet? I assessed one little boy whose mother told me he could play with his tablet in his own room and never interact with his older brother because his older brother was busy in his own room playing with his own tablet. They were three and six years old.

Other children may be attending day care and staying there a considerable amount of time until their parent(s) arrive to pick them up. They do not get to experience any alone time or downtime, and if it is quiet time, it is quiet time with twelve others!

We, and our children, need to find ways to self-regulate. We need to find ways to create quiet times, and silence, to bring balance into our lives. We need to have moments of quietness where we can observe our thoughts and not always react to them.

By using a variety of calming and/or invigorating strategies in this book, you can bring peace, tranquility, happiness, and health to your own body and to children in your care, which leads to success.

I now bring you *7 Strategies for Raising Calm, Inspired, and Successful Children.* I look forward to your using this book to assist children in navigating their daily lives with clarity, balance, and peace, using breathing, affirmations, touch, mindfulness, laughter, movement, and song to carry them through their lifelong experiences with joy, resiliency, and calmness to live inspired and successful lives.

Your Instant Insights...

- We live in a high-tech environment that does not offer us much quiet time.
- Scientific studies support the benefits of mind-body exercises.
- Calming activities lead to greater focus, productivity, and success.

Calming Your Child Through Breathing

"Feelings come and go like clouds in a windy sky. Conscious breathing is my anchor. "

-Thich Nhat Hanh

Breathing is such an important aspect of life—we perish without it—and yet so many take breathing for granted. I remember when I was about seven years of age and had a round hard piece of candy lodged in my windpipe. As I ran up the stairs, turning blue, I found my mother in the kitchen. She took one look at me and hit my back as hard as she could (something they tell you NOT to do in CPR class). Out came the candy, rolling across the kitchen floor. I thanked my mother for saving my life and realized then the importance of breathing (and of mothers!).

Children can use breath to become calmer and more focused. Breath takes you **FAR** to becoming

- **F**ocused
- **A**lert
- **R**elaxed

How does this happen?

When you or your child is feeling stressed, it is not easy to breathe deeply. You can feel as if an elephant is on your chest or like there's a belt buckled tightly around your waist constricting you, like you're wearing size 2 pants when you really are a size 6.

Most often we engage in shallow breathing, but bringing more oxygen into your brain can help calm your brain, reduce anxiety levels, strengthen your immune system, and uplift your spirits. You may not have control over how much traffic you have to drive through to get to your house or how hot the weather may be, but knowing how to utilize the para-sympathetic part of your nervous system (PNS) can effect change on how you and your child feel, and how you handle stress. When anyone is anxious, scared, or confused, the "fight, flight, freeze, or faint" state occurs. With "tummy breathing," the "fight, flight, freeze, or faint" cannot occur at the same time.

Calming Your Child through Breathing Activities:

1. **Tummy Breathing** – Breathing with your "tummy" and not your chest is a special way you and your child get rid of stress and tension in your bodies. When your body is calm, so is your mind. This exercise can be done while lying down, but if you need to breathe just where you are, that will work also. Remember, it is best to teach this relaxation breath when you and/or your child are not stressed or agitated. Have your child place a hand on the tummy (below the belly button) and one on the chest. Breathe in through the nose for about eight to ten seconds. Hold the breath for eight to ten seconds, and then breathe out the mouth for eight to ten seconds. You can close your eyes and feel the movement, in and out. Repeat this one or two more times.

   I like to sing this song to children about their tummy breath.

   Breathe in through your nose
   And up from your toes, and
   Simply let the jitters go!

You can also place a stuffed animal or soft pillow on your child's tummy and watch it rise as a deep breath is taken and fills the tummy with air. Watch the stuffed animal or soft pillow lower when the air is being blown out of the tummy. Props provide a visual clue, which is so helpful with young children.

2. **Smell the flowers and blow the dandelions** – Another image that works well is a garden of flowers. Let your child see himself in a garden of flowers—all different bright, cheery colors of reds, greens, yellows, and oranges. Each child takes a deep breath and smells the flowers for eight to ten seconds. Hold that breath for eight to ten seconds and then blow the air out the mouth as if blowing dandelions all over the meadow. This visualization offers an alternative picture of what the breath will look like, and how the dandelions can be blown. You might actually begin the exercise by bringing in some fresh flowers, and each child can smell the fragrance. Then share the dandelion and have each child watch as you blow, or if you have enough dandelions, let each child blow, and watch the dandelion fairy dust spread through the air.

3. **Breathe in the scent of a chocolate cake and blow out the lit birthday**

candles – Each day is a birthday and a time for celebration, so why not choose to use the imagery of a lovely, aromatic chocolate or strawberry cake (or use the flavors and aromas that your child likes the best)? We use the same idea about full tummy breathing, only this time when you breathe in, you will breathe in the smell of the delicious chocolate cake or strawberry frosting. Breathe in for eight to ten seconds, hold the breath for eight to ten seconds, and then blow out the birthday candles for eight to ten seconds. What could be better than celebrating a birthday?

Your Instant Insights...

- Anxiety brings on breath holding, hyperventilation, constricted breathing, and shortness of breath.

- Using deep breathing causes a reflex stimulation of the parasympathetic nervous system that triggers relaxation by relaxing muscles and reducing our heart rate.

- Your amygdala (fight, flight, freeze, faint) section of the brain is not activated when you are engaged in deep tummy breathing, which quiets your mind and relaxes your body.

Saying It's So with Your Child through Affirmations

"When you speak and affirm, you are creating a verbal contract with yourself"

-Bryant McGill

Wouldn't it be wonderful if you could teach your children how to say positive things about themselves? How often do you find yourself listening to negative things you say inside your own head? Well, Dr. Kathleen Hall, founder of the Stress Institute and the Mindful Living Network, asks, "How would you feel if you knew that by saying something positive, about yourself and your life, preferably out loud, you could alter the neurochemical reaction that affects your mental, physical and spiritual health?" I'd say, "Count me in!"

According to Dr. Edmund Jacobson, founder of Progressive Muscle Relaxation and the introducer of psychosomatic medicine, the subconscious mind plays a significant role in the actualization of our life and manifestation of our desires. He stated, "What we believe about ourselves at a subconscious level can have significant impact on our life." (1974). Our children, then, can use positive affirmations too, as a way to achieve their dreams and gain success.

New scientific data confirms this in a National Institute of Health study by distinguished psychologist J. David Creswell, and others, which showed how chronically stressed individuals who used affirmations, statements that something is true, boosted their problem solving, leading the way to show how self-affirmation can boost academic achievement in school settings (2013).

The mind does not know the difference between a statement that you are saying and a positive belief statement that is created to bring a truth into your life. For example, you can say, "I am beautiful!" and believe that to be true. You will walk like you are beautiful and talk as if you are beautiful. Your eyes will glisten like beautiful stars in the beauty of the night, and people who may never have looked at you will look at you now and want to know you. You are affirming your beauty as a truth and believing "I am beautiful!" Others who don't know you will want to know you, and others who know you will wonder what you have done that has left a spell on them.

Self-affirmations are positive tools used to assist with problem solving under stress. Children need ways to believe positive things themselves and build confidence. Using affirmations can build children up and help them believe that all things are possible and cast self-doubt aside. A three-year-old who uses the words "I can't" may be reflecting self-doubt and lack of confidence. By using affirmations such as, "I can" or "I am able to _____," the child can be brought to new heights. The positive affirmations may serve as a confidence booster so that the things they hear about themselves are more positive and open to possibilities and not to defeat.

A teacher told me about a five-year-old boy in her class who was timid and shy. He didn't make friends easily. She began using positive affirmations and having him repeat them. In a few weeks, he was playing with others and feeling happy. What was the affirmation he used? "I make friends easily!"

I also know a sixty-five-year-old grandmother who recites affirmations too, and she looks so youthful that people mistake her for being ten years younger. Her affirmation is "I am getting younger each day."

Affirmations can be used with young children (ages three to seven), adolescents, and adults. For a three-year-old, keep the affirmation about three words long. The affirmation can be longer for a seven-year-old.

"Saying It's So" with Your Child through Affirmation Activities:

Some sample affirmations that can be said aloud with a strong, happy voice when your child gets up each morning or arrives at school (actually, you can say them too!) are the following:

- I am happy, I am grateful (for this day).
- I am smart.
- I am ready.
- I love my family.
- I am joyful.
- I am friendly (and make friends easily).
- I am a miracle.
- I am able.

Some simple affirmations that can be spoken in a strong, happy, loving voice with your child before going to sleep each night include the following:

- I am grateful (for a beautiful day).
- I am blessed.
- I am loved.
- I believe in me.
- I am happy.
- I am content.
- I sleep easily.
- I appreciate me (and my family).

At home, in school, or in the community, stressful situations may occur. Let the child use an inner voice when surrounded by other people. In a calm, happy voice, say aloud any of the following:

- I am relaxed.
- I am calm.
- I am ready.
- I see good (in everyone).
- I find the beauty (in everything).
- I am friendly.
- I am worthy (of love).
- I accept myself.

The language used should be age appropriate, positive, and worded in the present tense, as though the situation already exists. Starting the affirmation with "I am ..." or using the present tense "I see ..." or "I find ..." is vital to believing the affirmation has already occurred. It is not something that will happen in the future. It is an affirmation of something that is occurring in the present. Each child experiences this belief in the present.

Using affirmations alone may not have the most impact by itself, so another helpful strategy includes other forms of relaxation and mindfulness to the affirmations. Some also use tapping (also known as EFT or Emotional Freedom Techniques) with affirmations.

Your Instant Insights...

- You can teach children, as young as three years of age, positive affirmations.

- By saying something positive about yourself and your life out loud, you alter the neurochemical reaction that affects your mental, physical, and spiritual health.

- The mind does not know the difference between a statement that you are saying and a positive belief statement that is created to bring TRUTH into your life.

Connecting with Your Child Through Touch

"Touch to survive, massage to thrive!"
\- Dr. Elaine Fogel Schneider

We all come into this world dressed only in our skin! Through our body's largest organ, the skin, we learn about ourselves and the world in which we live. Touch is the first sense to develop in utero, and it is a child's first means of communication. Professor Sir Michael Rutter, leader of the Romanian and English Adoptees Study Team, classic study of Romanian orphans showed that children in Romanian orphanages achieved only half their ordinary height because of extreme forms of touch deprivation, and their emotional and cognitive development were also significantly delayed by the lack of physical stimulation (1998).

The skin is made of the same cells as the brain; consequently, your body is the gateway to your mind. When you lovingly touch and massage your babies and children (and anyone else, for that matter), it is as if you are massaging their brain! You are releasing "feel-good" hormones (serotonin, melatonin, and oxytocin), sending nurturing messages throughout the body. You are also reducing the "stress" hormone cortisol. With faster, brisker movements, you can also energize weak muscle tone. The amygdala in the brain relaxes with the sense of nurturing touch, reducing the "fight, flight, freeze, and faint" reaction.

Connecting with Your Child through Touch Activities:

1. **Feel So Good** – A parent contacted me to say her son was starting preschool and was frightened. She wanted a way to connect with him. Using the TouchTime® ABCs in AWE (Attune, Breathe, Communicate in Acknowledgment, Wonderment, and Enjoyment)—first relaxing herself and with his permission—she massaged his shoulders and back for several minutes. She used firm, gentle strokes, kneading his shoulders and the back of his neck. She felt him relax under her touch. She kept her hands on his back with intentional touch for about ten seconds. Then, removing her

hands, she kissed him. Both parent and child were more relaxed. It was a win-win situation, and one that carried her son throughout the day. When he came home from school, he saw his mother dragging a bit and asked her, "Mom, do you want a massage?"

TouchTime® is a massage program I started over fifteen years ago for parents, health-care providers and teachers who have young children or who work with young children. Adults learn the many what's and how's of TouchTime®, i.e., The ABCs in AWE, 4 Pillars of Care, Touch Signatures,™ massage preparation, contraindications, reading readiness cues i.e., quiet alert readiness state, or "touchable moments." (See my book, *Massaging Your Baby- The Joy of TouchTime* for many more fun activities and songs.

My free *Baby Massage Basics App* for iPhones or iPads is also available online.)

2. **Quesadillas, anyone?** – Parents and health-care professionals have asked me what to do for toddlers, preschoolers, and children in early elementary grades who wouldn't "sit still" for an ordinary massage. Toddler Plus TouchTime® was created for older children, using many fun massage activities on children's backs while clothing stays on! A child's back

is massaged by making a "quesadilla" or "spring roll" or having a "car wash." Permission is received with respect; parents and/or professionals use the ABCs in AWE and; massage occurs through clothing.

Make a delicious quesadilla: Child lies on the soft floor, facedown, and gives permission to touch his back. Adult or other child takes a tummy breath to reduce any stress they have. They use fingertips and firmly and gently start massaging at the base of the neck and out to the shoulders, sweeping down to the waist with both hands. As you are massaging, you use your words to problem solve: "Do you want a corn or a flour quesadilla? What do you want to go inside your quesadilla?" First, open up the soft shell and smooth it around your child's back. "What else goes in?" You can pretend to add tomatoes, avocado, etc., and use a chopping motion to chop up the fillings. "What else do you want?" "Chicken." Make little circles on his back. "Cheese!" Then use a sprinkling motion on your child's back for the cheese. When they say "no," you can smooth the quesadilla with both hands, doing a combing motion down the back, and then hold your hands on the back of your child and say, "It's cooking in the oven and getting warm." Hold your hands on the back intentionally for a few more seconds and say, "Ding! Ding! Ding! The quesadilla is ready!" Lift your hands off your child's back. Have fun! And thank each other for the massage. For readers of this book, you can find more fun activities at www.askdrelaine.com.

3. **Family Commercial Break** – Most everybody has one television or more. Why not use the commercial breaks as a way to connect with your family in the comfort of your home? Have your natural oils ready. Foot massages or hand massages are wonderful during the commercial breaks. Permission, of course, is always given and received, and you have taken a few breaths to relax yourself. Let the massage begin!

Your Instant Insights...

- Your skin is the largest organ in your body and has a multiplicity of functions.

- Touch is not a frill. It is a biological necessity without which failure to thrive in infants may occur in addition to intellectual impairments.

- A nurturing touch increases "feel-good hormones" (oxytocin, serotonin, and melatonin) and reduces the "stress hormone" cortisol.

Being Here Now with Your Child Through Mindfulness

*"Refuge to man is the mind, refuge to
the mind is mindfulness."*

\- Buddha

According to Jon Kabat-Zinn, Professor of Medicine Emeritus, and creator of the Stress Reduction Clinic and the Center for Mindfulness in Medicine, Health Care, and Society at the University of Massachusetts Medical School, mindfulness is "the awareness that emerges through paying attention on purpose, in the present moment, and nonjudgmentally to the unfolding of experiences moment by moment."

The goal of mindfulness is to have an increased awareness of the present moment. It requires that we slow down and learn to bring stillness to our busy minds (Kidsactivitiesblog.com). It's like the time you find yourself standing at the shore, looking out at the horizon, and hearing, almost for the first time the crescendo of a wave coming into the beach, and then going back out to sea. It's like your catching your own breath, the moment between the ebb and flow, and in that quiet moment you find peace and calmness. When we bring stillness to our busy minds, then we do not react to our thoughts or busy minds, we can choose our behaviors.

"I'm not my thoughts" can change the way children view themselves, from early years into teen years when the burden of anxiety and fitting in can be a bit much for anybody.

Families are so busy—getting to school, getting to work, meeting deadlines—yet it is so important to make the time to slow down and be in a quiet place where you can observe your breath, feel calm, and reduce the "alert" state of your amygdala. (The amygdala is an almond-shaped mass of gray matter in the front part of the temporal lobe of the cerebrum that is part of the limbic system and is involved in giving you information about and expression of emotions, especially the four Fs of *fight, flight, freeze,* and *faint.*)

The amygdala is reactive to stress and fear and raises its head of anxiety and protection, like in the days when people hunted for food and ran away from tigers. So even though you do not see the activities as the sources of your anxiety or fright, your body responds as if the enemy is closing in on you or threatening your very being—and oftentimes, there is no enemy other than yourself!

One child causes the toilet to back up by throwing too much toilet paper into the bowl, while another child is screaming because a wheel came off their toy truck, and your thermostat is on fire. When you can take a deep breath and label the behaviors, you can turn down the amygdala, the fear center of the brain. Now your prefrontal cortex, the place responsible for reasoning, can become more present to the situation at hand. You might even label the activities as "chaotic" or "humorous," and you can be more peaceful in your way of responding to the issues at hand.

Mindfulness is beneficial to the child and parent, caregiver, teacher, or grandparent too! Mindfulness is a way for children to notice that in addition to things outside their bodies (like the sun, the Earth, the moon, food trucks, or ice cream trucks), there are thoughts and movements flowing through their own body. By stopping in time, a child pays attention to himself in addition to things outside himself.

Being Here Now with Your Child through Mindfulness Activities:

1. **Vibrating Drum** – Each child listens to the sound of a vibrating drum. When he can no longer hear the sound of the beating drum, he raises a hand. When the vibrating drum stops, keeping eyes closed, listen to the other sounds in the environment. With preschoolers, I can have them keep their eyes closed for up to fifteen to thirty seconds. Older children can keep their eyes closed longer and continue listening to other sounds in the environment. When it is time to open their eyes, ask what other sounds they heard. I love to do this outdoors too, so the children can hear the sounds of birds, airplanes, mowers, and trucks, to name a few.

2. **Make a movie** – Children get to focus attention on themselves, as if they're making a movie and reporting what they did in the morning or throughout the day. See if they can get to more and more details so that the child can remember more and more minute details of each day.

3. **Relax yourself** – Tightening and relaxing muscles progressively was introduced by Dr. Edmund Jacobsen almost one hundred years ago. Young children can sit on a chair or lie on the floor, tightening up muscles, as tight as they can go, and then relaxing

the muscles. I like to use a rubber band to show the children how the rubber band is pulled tight, and then how it releases and relaxes into something soft. I always get permission to start, and when I hear "yes," we begin with making a fist, as tight as it will go, and then relax it. Flex toes backwards and tighten up the legs up to the thighs, into the buttocks and hips, and relax. Move on to the tummy and tighten the abdomen, then relax. Move up to the chest, shoulders, and down the arms to the hands; make fists with the hands and tighten up their faces; hold all of those places in the body tightly, then relax each body part simultaneously, with an exhalation through the mouth. When the body is engaged in this relaxation exercise, the mind and body are in the present.

Your Instant Insights...

- Evidence supports the notion that mindfulness is an effective way of building resiliency in children and promoting positive habits of mind and body.

- Mindfulness provides exceptional lifelong skills for well-being and happiness that calm, refocus energy, and increase attention, enhancing concentration, memory, and learning, as well as facilitating a more productive and relaxed, less anxious and stressful environment.

- Mindfulness allows the mind to observe thoughts, feelings, sensations, and perceptions without judgment, and without reaction while being in the present moment.

Going on a Vacation with Your Child Through Laughter

"Laughter is the shortest distance between two people."

- Victor Borge

Laughter is such an important part of life. Children are naturally happy and carefree. Why then would you need to teach them how to laugh? Oftentimes parents feel strange playing with their children. Sometimes the rules of the house don't allow for much humor. A parent may be overly protective and solemn in their approach to parenting. Parents may be stressed by their responsibilities of raising children, not allowing time for humor. Joel Osteen, Internationally -known pastor of the Lakewood Church said, "If you have children at home, there is no reason you shouldn't be laughing all through the day. Don't get so caught up in the pressures of raising your children that you don't take the time to enjoy them" (2016). The child may be so overscheduled with extracurricular activities that laughing is not an option!

We connect through humor. Humor fosters higher levels of creative thinking, which is important to a child's social and emotional development. Children laugh about 400 times a day as compared to an adult's fifteen times. As a child gets older, the laughter continues to decrease. What makes something funny? Something has to be humorous. Just the other day I was sitting with my grandchildren looking at the photos on my iPhone since they wanted me to show them the Goodyear Blimp pictures. (When I drive from my home to their home, I pass the home of the Goodyear Blimp. I usually take a photo of the blimp sitting on the ground.)

Having fun with my grandchildren, aged eighteen months and almost four years, I showed them the photo of the blimp, and then I pretended to make a mistake and showed them the wrong photo, a photo of my foot, or a photo of the door handle in my car. When I showed them the incorrect photo, I said, "Oh, here's the blimp." They would both laugh hysterically and say, "No, GeeyGeey, that's not the blimp!" Then I would show them the blimp photo, and then the next time I would pretend to make a mistake and show them the door handle in my car, and that would make them laugh hysterically again. My daughter asked, "What's so funny?" and my son-in-law was so captivated by this he took a photo of this interchange. We three were totally connected, in the moment, laughing hysterically.

The benefits of laughter have been scientifically proven. Scientists have studied brain waves and how they change the disposition in the brain's happy centers. Harvard Medical School began these studies in the 1970s, and other universities followed. Laughter releases serotonin in the brain, which brings relaxation and "feel-good" hormones. Endorphins—hormones secreted by the brain and nervous system that have a number of physiological functions—activate the body's opiate receptors, causing an analgesic effect. Endorphins reduce the sensation of pain and stimulate positive emotion. Their release is critical for stress relief, and therefore for our mental health. Researchers at Loma Linda University in California found that participants who had laughed for twenty minutes showed benefits with memory recall, and considerably lower levels of cortisol, the "stress hormone."

Blood flow increases in the brain when children laugh. Tension can be released, and humor increases the brain's receptivity to learning. Laughter increases the oxygenation of the organs, boosts circulation, and contributes to an overall sense of well-being.

Research shows that laughter enhances children's intellectual, social, and emotional development. I add that it enhances a child's ability to be mindfully in the moment and increases their receptivity to learning. Where there is no judgment and playfulness prevails, laughter overtakes the body where nothing matters but the laughter and silliness of the moment. According to the late comedian Milton Berle, "Laughter is the vacation you give yourself!"

In their "Top Ten Benefits of Humor," Villanova University stated that just as studies show the positive effects of smiling occur whether the smile is fake or real, faked laughter also provides the benefits mentioned above.

Going on a Vacation with Your Child Through Laughter Activities:

1. **Fake it, till you make it!** Whether you have reason to laugh, make it happen. Laugh at the way the water goes down the drain, or the way a balloon floats into the sky. Make something up that's funny. Laugh for the sake of laughing. Stay with the laughter for one minute and become happier.

2. **Smile as big as you can! Laugh as loudly as you can!** The body doesn't know whether the smile is a smile that is felt or one that is being put on. So put a smile on your face each morning, at home, at school, in the community, and start the day off with a smile. Whenever needed, remind children to smile, and continue to smile throughout the day. You can smile and laugh at breakfast, lunch, and dinner. Laugh in the classroom, at home, in the community, and throughout the day. Laugh as loudly as you can!

3. **Name that Laugh!** Tape different people laughing in your family (or in a classroom) and see if you can match the person with his or her laugh! Then try to imitate the laugh.

Your Instant Insights...

- Laughing together is a way to connect in the moment.

- Children who can appreciate and share humor are better liked by their peers and better able to handle difficulties of childhood.

- Research shows children with a well-developed sense of humor are happier and more optimistic, better able to cope with challenges, have higher self-esteem, are likely to be less depressed, and may have more resistance to illness or physical problems.

Freeing Your Child Through Movement and Music

"Where words leave off, music begins."
- Heinrich Heine

"Existence is movement."
- Rudolf Laban

"Dance is the hidden language of the soul."
- Martha Graham

"The arts are the connective tissue that holds our spirits intact."
- Mimi Brodsky Chenfeld

I can remember when I was around four years of age, running barefooted and leaping through space, holding a scarf above my head, under the eyes of a creative movement instructor (and my mother). A sense of freedom came over me, and the spirit moved me. Hearing the beating of a drum, engaged in my own freedom dance, I could have run and danced forever. In that moment of feeling free as the wind, I felt a connection with creativity and at peace in the moment. I felt like a butterfly, out of my cocoon, taking flight.

In the moment, you become one with the solution and have no worry or thought of what you are going to wear tomorrow to school, or why you are not happy about the color of the mac-and-cheese box. There is no room for those kinds of thoughts as you purposefully figure out problems and solve the simplest direction of moving from one part of the room to another without touching another child, or moving like a spider, or a caterpillar, or snake, slithering along the floor.

We know that children do well with structure and rules. What we may not know is that moving in space without set rules, but moving through space the way one's own body wants to move, with ways of maneuvering between other children (or yourself) can lead to self-discipline, positive self-image, and body awareness.

Children learn to control their bodies when they change direction and speed. Moving in a shared space teaches social skills while children also learn to take turns and find a solution to a question. Solving problems in this way can be freeing and lead to one's creativity and freedom of expression. Words are not the only way we can communicate.

Neuroscientist Carla Hannaford explains that begin-ning in infancy, physical movement plays a vital role in the creation of the nerve cell networks that are at the core of learning. An infant's brain is full of brain cells that are making connections, very much so during the first three years of life. If these brain cell connections are made repeatedly, they become permanent, but if they are not performed repeatedly, they are lost. "Movement activates the neural wiring throughout the body, the whole body, and not just the brain, and is an instrument of learning. (2005).

Early music training develops brain areas involved in language and reasoning—the left hemisphere and prefrontal cortex. The relaxing effect music has on the body can relax your child, and when stress is reduced, more learning can occur. You lose "yourself" and find "yourself" in the rhythm and the harmonics of the moment.

Self-esteem is a by-product of self-expression, and you can sense improved self-esteem.

Educationally, scientists explain how music helps your child gain skills in math, short-term memory, and long-term memory, and how it can enhance skills needed for education and social interaction, but how does it integrate the mind and body and bring calm to your child?

The National Association of the Education of Young Children (NAEYC), with Connie Bergstein Dow, support creative dance as a way for children to come up with questions and solutions, nurturing self-expression and creativity. Dr. John Ratey, clinical professor of psychiatry at Harvard Medical School, further stated, "Exercise{movement} improves learning on three levels: first, it optimizes your mindset to improve alertness, attention, and motivation; second it prepares and encourages nerve cells to bind to one another which is the cellular basis for logging in new information; and third it spurs the development of new nerve cells from stem cells in the hippocampus" (2008). (The hippocampus is part of the brain involved in emotions, learning and memory formation.)

Freeing Your Child through Movement and Music Activities:

1. **A Musical Band** – Use musical instruments and make a musical band. Let your child create rhythms that stir your child, and let your child march around the room or float

like a cloud, creating a song all their own. Change the instruments and make another song. Encourage your child to use as many instruments as they would like—a bell, a drum, etc.

2. **Move to the Beat** – Use musical instruments to make a beat and move your body to the beat. You can make the sound loud and make a big movement. You can make the sound soft and make a small movement. You can make a loud sound and a little movement, or a soft sound and a big movement. Explore different sounds and ways little bodies can move, changing shapes and strength.

Find out how your child feels in the moment. Ask questions about which movements they liked. When you are in the moment, you are present to the experience and not wondering about the future or the past. (More activities are free for you to download on my website www. askdrelaine.com.)

3. **Monkey See, Monkey Do** – Use music and create movements, and let your child imitate your movement (or in a group, imitate a leader's movement). You might pretend you're stirring a big pot of spaghetti. Then let someone else lead, and your child follows that leader. For older children, you can ask, "Do you like to lead

or follow?" For younger children, have the fun of imitation without judgment.

Your Instant Insights...

- Creative arts optimize your mindset to improve alertness, attention, and motivation, encouraging nerve cells to bind to one another, the cellular basis for logging in new information.

- Creative arts spur new nerve cells to come up with questions and solutions.

- Making music and moving creatively have a relaxing effect on the body, reducing stress hormones.

Understanding Your Child through Brain-Based Research – A GetREAL Now™ (Get Ready Everyone and Learn Now) Approach

"Mindfulness about the present is also about being real."

- Krista Tippett

GetREAL Now™ is the name of a program I developed that combines a number of awareness and self-regulation strategies for daily use with children and their parents/caregivers to bring harmony, happiness, health, and calmness to one's life, leading to academic and personal success. In the moment of quiet alertness, optimum learning occurs.

Early experiences affect the development of brain architecture, which provides the foundation for all future learning, behavior, and health. "An environment of relationships is crucial for development of a child's brain architecture which lays the foundation for later outcomes such as academic performance, mental health, and interpersonal skills" (National Scientific Council on the Developing Child, 2004). The serve and return (being responsive to a child's needs and cues, i.e., as in the TouchTime® program) established by parents and extended family members with infants shapes the circuitry.

As a child grows with this consistent relational foundation, so does their brain. When toxic stress occurs and affects the outpouring of physiological stress reactions (i.e., increased heart rate, increased inflammation, and putting the body into a "fight, flight, freeze or faint" mode in the limbic system), then the ability for self-regulation is poor, learning is at risk—as is the developing brain—and your child suffers.

According to Daniel J. Siegel, professor of clinical psychiatry at UCLA School of Medicine and Executive Director of The Mindsight Institute, the most exciting scientific discoveries of the last twenty years show how scientists who once thought that early experiences stimulated the brain have discovered that early experiences structure and shape the brain. (1999).

Other researchers, Aamodt and Wang, with over forty years of experience have shared the early stages of discovery about the footprints on the genome, whereby a child's experiences can cause permanent changes to their DNA and thus effect change to their own future generation's genes. For example, experimental mice who thrived for two weeks in an enriched environment learned more easily when adults, and so did their offspring even when the offspring were raised in a non-enriched environment. (2011).

Your child's brain needs intervention to build brain circuitry. When you build from the brain up, the circuits are made and continue to grow. Neuroscience has shown that we can grow new connections throughout our lives, or if we don't use our connections, as scientists like to say, we must "use it or lose it!"

You can assist in building a strong foundation for your child, or a weak foundation. In the rich nurturing of a relationship, the foundation is strong, and your child's brain thrives. In a toxic situation, brain cells can wither away and die.

Brain circuitry is highly integrated. Children are best prepared for school with an integration approach. Scientific evidence shows how stimulating and responsive intervention builds a strong foundation for effective learning. What can undermine the brain circuitry and affect your child's growth and development? Toxic stress undermines the brain circuitry. Toxic stress also undermines the acquisition of skills and interrupts skills already learned.

And yet it is scientifically proven that stress occurs in everyone's life. It is how we deal with stress that will lead to how we grow or fail to grow. The de-stressing activities shown to you in this book are ways to ward off toxic stress and ensure a healthier lifestyle for your children and your children's children, and generations to come.

Other scientific revelations show us how nature and nurture have "stopped fighting" and are seen now under a different light. Both play vital roles in the development of children, and so it is not singly the genetics you are born with that make you who you are; it is also the way you are nurtured and your experiences that will shape you. Even if scholars do not unravel all the nuances, "It is for certain, stated Aamodt and Wang, that neither genetic inheritance nor environmental conditions alone are destiny for any child."

You are the most important person in your child's life. You are the role model upon which your child learns about the world and how to navigate through it. Using the strategies of deep breathing, self-affirmations, touch, mindfulness, laughter, movement and music will help grow your child's brain and bring homeostasis to your child.

Parenting children is its own reward, especially when you know that you are structuring your child's brain and future generations to come. The ability to regulate behavior is important for academic achievement and interpersonal success. Combining a variety of stress-reducing strategies as presented to you in this book and using them on an ongoing basis alters brain chemistry, develops your child's response to stress, and brings forward your child's optimum growth and development. It is wonderful to now have science back up what many of us intuitively knew was beneficial.

Here's a whimsical poem I wrote for you to share about "Quiet Alertness".

In the moment of quiet alertness,
Optimum learning takes place.
In the moment of quiet alertness,
I can sense even my own face.

The place responsible for so many senses,
The place responsible for seeing through lenses.
I can sense my ears,
Birds, planes, and trains, I hear.

I can sense my nose,
Smelling a rose.

I can feel my mouth, too,
And all that I can chew.

I can sense the place where
My thoughts begin,
And move,
Without a care.

In the moment of quiet alertness,
Any stress?
Any worries?
Any fear?

I do not react,
Rather, I observe.

In the moment of quiet alertness,
I am still.

Between the ebb and flow,
In the moment of quiet alertness,
I learn and I grow!

Your Instant Insights...

- Early experiences are built into our body.
- In the moment of quiet alertness, optimum learning takes place.
- A strong foundation for education achievements requires us to both stimulate minds and protect brains.

Conclusion...
Bringing It All Together for Your Child and You

Congratulations! You have taken a journey so that you can be the best parent/caregiver, educator, or health-care professional you can be for your children or for children in your care. Considering the busy lives you live and the stressors of daily living, I greatly appreciate your selecting this book and reading it to learn more about the many strategies you can use for raising calm, inspired, and successful children.

As a parent (or as an adult caring for a child), you are your child's first teacher. What does your child see you do when you want to calm yourself? How do you respond to events? What are the practices you follow to stay calm and happy?

In this book, I have included a variety of strategies so that you can pick and choose different ones that your child and you like. The activities are simple and easy to use with seven different categories for seven different days. You can vary them, or use the same ones over time. I've made them fun, quick, and powerful.

Just watching the amount of work and time you put into your own children, like my daughter and son-in-law, I know how valuable each moment is, each and every day. Although you may feel tired at the end of the day, your relationships with your children are forming the architecture of your child's brain. The pathways you are forming in your child's brain are affecting their future children and their future children's children. You are growing your child's brain, restructuring DNA, and by introducing breathing, affirmations, nurturing touch, mindfulness, laughter, and movement and music, you are creating a loving, trusting environment where relationships blossom, and upon which all future relationships will be based.

It is my dream that all children will be nurtured and loved and develop life skills so that they do not need to go through life stressed and uptight. It would be my biggest pleasure to know that families are better equipped to reduce stress in their own homes, and that educators and health-care professionals are better able to effect change in their students' lives.

It is important to notice which kinds of activities presented in this book are a good fit for your child because some children may not enjoy mindfulness experiences. Others may not enjoy affirmations. Encourage your child to practice the exercises, and if necessary, practice letting go. As in many interventions, it is vital to see which strategies work best. Responsiveness is critical to the growth and development of a child, and by using many of the strategies provided, you will be able to effect change.

Always acknowledge your child's efforts to use these strategies. Jackie, mother of Ruby and Mason, seven-year-old twins, also includes a success chart and stickers as a reward when her children use these strategies.

Emotional freedom technique (EFT, also known as tapping), mentioned previously, and Yoga are other methods of relaxation and mindfulness that have been shown beneficial for children, that reduce stress and negative energy, that prepare children for learning, and that facilitate optimum living. Nutrition also plays an important role in your child's calmness and success. You can go to my website http://askdrelaine.com for more information about these strategies.

The interaction between you and your children and other caregivers in the family or community is critical for your child's developing mind and ability to self-regulate. When children believe they can observe their thoughts and know that they are not their thoughts, and when children learn at an early age different ways to calm themselves so that they can focus and achieve their dreams, there is no limit on the successes they will achieve in their everyday life. Others may see problems; they will see solutions. Others may become easily frustrated when something doesn't go their way; they will be able to go with the flow. Others may sense themselves as victims; they will see themselves as victors.

You are a major ingredient in this developmental process of shaping your child's brain and, therefore, how your child responds to events. In the absence of responsive caregiving—or if responses are unreliable or inappropriate—the brain's architecture does not form as expected, which can lead to disparities in learning and behavior. Ultimately, genes and experiences work together to construct brain architecture (Harvard University Child Development).

Sharing the activities presented in this book with your child enables your child to discover ways of being that are healthy and can place them in the moment, so that they are more resilient as adults, and have a better attitude about life, whether by laughing with their problems, or dancing away their worries.

The ultimate goal for children is preparation for calm, inspired, successful lives where children are aware of their thoughts and their actions, while not necessarily reacting to them. Where children can learn to calm themselves, they will be ready to learn. If children can have a sense of humor and laugh at themselves, life will be easier too in handling different situations that arise, that may try to interfere with reaching goals.

Thank you for the opportunity to share this information with you. Let me hear back from you about how your children received the activities. Let me know what changes you have seen with your children and in your own lives too! If you have any questions, please send them to me at my Facebook page
https://www.facebook.com/askdrelaine for our community.

You can reach me also at:
info@askdrelaine.com.

About the Author

Dr. Elaine Fogel Schneider is an expert in the field of communication, (verbal and nonverbal, including touch), child development, and mind-body alternative health. She is an author, trainer, coach, and consultant, and one of the country's leading authorities on baby massage therapy. She holds a PhD in psychology and two master of arts degrees in the fields of speech-language pathology and dance/movement therapy, and is the founder of TouchTime®, devoted to enriching family connections and relationships, building healthy and happy families through the first language of communication, the language of touch. Dr. Schneider is also the founder of Community Therapies, Baby Steps, and GetREAL Now™, dedicated to promoting calmness and self-awareness in children.

In 1981, Dr. Schneider founded Community Therapies and Baby Steps, a comprehensive center-based and home-based family-centered early intervention program situated in the geographical areas of Antelope and Santa Clarita Valleys, California. These programs have served thousands of infants and toddlers, from birth to three years of age, and their families, and older children and adults, including children with autism, Down syndrome, premature birth conditions, cerebral palsy, and other special needs. Dr. Schneider has provided evaluations, therapeutic intervention, staff supervision, and parent training and education for more than thirty-five years. Under Dr. Schneider's leadership, Community Therapies has been named a Center of Excellence with the Los Angeles County Department of Mental Health.

Dr. Elaine is the author of three books, including *Massaging Your Baby: Effective Techniques for a Healthier, Happier, More Relaxed Child and Parent – The Joy of TouchTime™* translated into Chinese and Malay and an e-book of poetry, *Expressions From The Heart,* and co-author of *Pictures Please* by Harcourt Brace. Her articles have appeared in academic journals and in consumer publications, e.g., *Parent's Magazine, Child, Council for Exceptional Children,* and *Zero to Three.* She has produced an application, *Baby Massage Basics,* for iPhones and iPads, and soon for other smart phones. She has also been invited to write for various blogs and websites.

Dr. Schneider has appeared on national television as an expert in child and family issues, featured on The Learning Channel's *Slice of Life*, Time Warner and Fox News 11, and many radio shows.

Dr. Schneider is an expert in the area of child development. As an award-winning speech and language pathologist, she has also provided in-home and center-based therapeutic services for children and their families in a multidisciplinary team, she supervises speech and language pathology assistants, and serves as a consultant to Long Beach Unified preschool assessment team.

She is the longest-sitting governor appointee to the State of California's Early Start Interagency Coordinating Council (ICC) representing service providers; a TouchTime® instructor trainer for parents, healthcare providers, and other professionals; a consultant with Long Beach Unified School District's Pre School Assessment Team; and was previously a consultant for SEEDS (Supporting Early Education Delivery Systems) and a statewide trainer for WestEd Center for Early Intervention and Prevention.

Dr. Elaine is an invited speaker to many national and international conferences, presenting her work on Raising Healthy Kids, ETC-Early TouchTime® Communication for speech and language pathologists, touch and its role in communication and balancing a multi-generational life, and the importance of routine strategies to raise calm, inspired, and successful children.

Her articles have been published in popular national magazines, e.g., *Parents Magazine*, *Massage Magazine*, *Let's Live*, and other professional journals, and she has been referenced in textbooks and infant massage books. Dr. Schneider's article "The Power of Touch: Massage for Infants" first appeared in the peer-reviewed journal *Infants and Young Children* (1996) and laid the foundation for using infant massage in many early-intervention, birth-to-three programs throughout the country.

Dr. Schneider is a fellow of California Speech, Language and Hearing Association. She was awarded the Jynny Retsinger Award from the North Los Angeles County Regional Center for her service to children and families, and has received other national awards.

As one of the leading experts in the country on infant massage and early intervention, Dr. Schneider has been a keynote speaker and invited speaker for organizations such as Zero to Three, American Speech-Language and Hearing Association, California Speech-Language and Hearing Association, The International Association of Infant Massage, UNESCO, Head Start, Early Head Start, The Infant Development Association of California, the Center for the Improvement of Child Caring, and major school districts and preschools. She provides three-day trainings for individuals to become certified TouchTime® instructors.

Dr. Schneider is a practicing meditator of over thirty-eight years. She treats her life as a gift that she is grateful for, each and every day. She has participated in various higher-learning and self-awareness programs and studied with many masters of self-awareness and mindfulness, including but not limited to Nick Ortner of "the Tapping Solution," Landmark Education, Tony Robbins, Maharishi Mahesh Yogi's Transcendental Meditation (TM) program, Deepak Chopra's Primordial Sound Meditation, Jack Canfield, and Joel Osteen's prayer and hope affirmations.

She was a co-owner of DanceTheatre, a dance company in Coconut Grove, Florida, and performed modern dance professionally and trained educators on the art of dance and how to include creative movement in the classroom. She was also awarded a grant from Dade County Board of Education to bring creative movement into a school for children with special needs. She is committed to promoting successful children and families, in which children of all ages and their families thrive. Living in this busy world, Dr. Schneider began to provide workshops about the 7 Strategies for Raising Calm, Inspired, and Successful Children, including all the strategies she uses for herself to keep her life balanced, happy, and successful. She is a wife, mother, and loving grandmother and resides in Long Beach, California. You can visit her on her website at www.askdrelaine.com or her Facebook page, https://www.facebook.com/askdrelaine or contact her via e-mail at: drelaine@askdrelaine.com.

Other Books by this Author

Massaging Your Baby – The Joy of TouchTime – Effective Techniques for Happier, Healthier, and More Relaxed Children & Parents. (2006) New York: Square One Publishers.

Expressions from the Heart – A Collection of Poetry. Book II. (2016)

Expressions from the Heart – A Collection of Poetry. Book I. (1995)

Baby Massage Basics App for iPhones and iPads

Connect with the Author

Website:
http://AskDrElaine.com

Email:
drelaine@askdrelaine.com

Social Media:
Facebook:
https://www.facebook.com/askdrelaine

LinkedIn:
https://www.linkedincom/in/dr-elaine-fogel-schneider-3957642a

Twitter:
@askdrelaine

Instagram:
https://www.instagram/Dr. Elaine Fogel Schneider

Pinterest:
https://www.pinterest/elainefogelschneider

Google+:
https://plus.google.com/ElaineFogelSchneider/

Acknowledgements

I would like to thank all the parents and children who, over the years, have been my teachers and who have put their trust and confidence in me. I would also like to thank all the parents and professionals who asked questions and wanted more answers about their children, or the children they serve, who encouraged me to create programs to serve them.

I would also like to acknowledge my dear husband, Jack, for his love and kindness, and for being my stalwart during the time I spent writing this book. Since we were moving residences, many days I left him holding the "boxes," so to speak, and he stayed in the flow.

I would like to thank my beautiful "miracle daughter" Karli for allowing me to be the best mother I can be and loving me unconditionally, and now for allowing me to be the best "Geey Geey" I can be to my two beautiful grandchildren, Memphis and Finley, who make my heart happy with delight and make my spine tingle. They are the miracles I see daily, and the joy they bring me to "live in the now." They also inspire me to leave a legacy and let my voice be heard. To them and their children and their children's children, I am grateful to be able to make a difference in their worlds. Thanks also go out to my wonderful son-in-law, Hayden, for his laughter, his joy, and genuine caring.

There are too many friends to thank by name, but you know who you are, who inspired me, supported me, and leant a helping hand whenever I needed your touch, and when I thought I didn't need one at all.

Thanks also go out to the many teachers I have had along the way of my journey, who have given me the tools for my own calming.

Last, but not least, thanks to Robbin Simons and her team at Crescendo Publishing for making my dream a reality.

References

Introduction

Diamond, M., & Hopson, J. (1998). *Magic trees of the mind: How to nurture your child's intelligence, creativity, and healthy emotions from birth through adolescence.* New York: Dutton.

Kroger, W, M.D., in Fezler, PhD. (1980). *Just Imagine: A Guide to Materialization Using Imagery.* New York: Laurida.

Nummenmaa, L., Glerean, E., Hari, R., Hietanen, R. *Bodily Maps of Emotions.* www.pmas.org/tcgi/801/10.1973/1321664111 retrieved 2/1/2016.

Siegel, D.J. (1999). *The Developing Mind.* New York: Guilford Press.

Tennant, V. (2003). *Calming Ourselves in Stressful Moments, Helping Young Children and their Caregivers Manage Stress.* Comprehensive Health Education Foundation.

Calming Your Child through Breathing Activities

Jacobson, E. *Progressive Relaxation.* (1974). Chicago: The University of Chicago Press, Midway Reprint.

Schneider, E.F. (2006) *Massaging Your Baby-The Joy of TouchTime* ®Effective *Techniques for a Healthier, Happier, More Relaxed Child & Parent.* New York: Square One Publishers.

Siegel, D.J. (1999). *The Developing Mind.* New York: Guilford Press.

Saying It's So with Your Child through Affirmation

Affirmations in Action for Kids. http://yokid. org/resources/activities/affirmations.

Creswell, DJ, Dulcher, JM, Klein, W., Harris, P., Levine, J. "Self-Affirmation Improves Problem-Solving Under Stress" http://dz.doi.org/10.137/ journal pone 00262593.

Hall, K. CEO and Founder of Stress Institute and Mindful Living Network. www.drkathleenhull. com.

Jacobson, W.E., *How Affirmations Can Improve Your Life and Relationships. Huffpost Healthy Living*, August 9, 2011.

Legault, L, Al-Khindi, T., Inzlicht, MN. (2012). Preserving Integrity in the Face of Performance Threat: Self-Affirmation Enhances Neurophysiological Responsiveness to Errors". *Psychological Science*, 23, 1455-1460.

Ortner, N. (2013). *The Tapping Solution*. India: Hay House, 2013.

"Self-Affirmation Enhances Performance, Makes Us Receptive to Our Mistakes". http://www.psychologicalscience.org/index.phpnews,releases/self-affirmations.

Shermand, D.K., Cohen, G.L. (2006). "The Psychology of Self-Defense: Self Affirmation Theory" in M.P. Zanna (ed) Advances in Experimental Social Psychology. Vol 38, San Diego Academic Press, 183-242.

Williams, R. "Do Self-Affirmations Work? A Revisit" (May 5. 2013). https://www.psychologytoday. Com/blog/wired-success/201.305/do-self-affirmations-work-revisit.

Connecting Your Child through Touch

Aamodt, S., and Wang, S. (2011). *Welcome to your Child's Brain*. New York: MJF Books.

Perry, Bruce, M.D., Ph.D., "The Power of Early Childhood." Kaiser Health Foundation Leadership Foundation, 2005.

Rutter. M. and he ERA study team (1998). Development catch-up, and deficit following adoptions after severe global early privation. *Journal of Child Psychiatry*. 39 (4). 465-476.

Schneider, E.F. *Massaging Your Baby-The Joy of TouchTime® Effective Techniques for a Healthier, Happier and Relaxed Child & Parent.* New York: Square One Publishers, 2006.

Schneider, E.F. (2010) *Baby Massage Basics*, iPhone Application/iPad Application.

Schneider, E.F., and Patterson, P. (Dec. 5, 2010) "You've Got That Magic Touch: Integrating the Sense of Touch into Early Childhood Services. *Young Exceptional Children Division for Early Childhood*. 17-27.

Schneider, E.F., and Patterson P. (2011) "Touch Therapy Integrating the Senses of Touch." Autism Conference of America, Pasadena, Ca.

Being Here Now through Mindfulness

Brown, K.W., Ryan, R.M. the Benefits of Being Present Mindfulness and Its Role in Psychological Well-Being. *Journal of Personality and Social Psychology* (84)(4) 822848.

Hibberd, J, Usmer, J. (2015). *This Book Will Make You Mindful*. New York: Hachette Book Group.

Hooker, KE., Fodor, IE. (2008). *Teaching Mindfulness to Children*. 12(1). 75-91.

Kabat-Zinn, J., Williams, M. (Eds). (2013) *Mindfulness: Diverse Perspectives on its Meaning, Origins, and Applications.* New York: Routledge.

Reza, A, Chaiasbianhow, C., and Jahari, G. *Effect of Mindfulness Practices on Executive Functions of Elementary School Students.* Nov. 2015, 9-18.

Saltzman, A., and Santorelli, S. (2014) *A Still Quiet Place*. Oakland, Ca: New Harbinger Publications.

Siegel, DJ. (1999). *The Developing Mind*. New York: Guilford Press.

Going on Vacation with Your Child through Laughter

Berk. A. (2008). Anticipating A Laugh Reduces Our Stress Hormones, Study Shows. *American Physiological Society.*

Church, EB. *Encouraging Your Child's Sense of Humor. Let's Get the Bad Guys*. Kids.org.

Gorman, J. Scientists Hint at Why Laughter Feels So Good. *New York Times.* September 13, 2011.

McGee, P. (2013). *Humor and Child Development*, New York: Routledge.

Miller, S A., Church, E.B, and Poole, C. Ages and Stages: Don't Forget to Laugh – The Importance of Humor In www.positiveparents.com.

Osteen, Joel. Joel and Victoria Osteen Ministries. www.joelosteen.com and www. PositiveParenting.com.

Skerrett, P. (2010). Laugh and be thankful - it's good for the heart. *Harvard Health Publications*, Harvard Medical School.

Freeing Your Child through Movement and Music

Bergstein Dow, C. MFA. *Young Children and Movement: The Power of Creative Dance. (National Association of the Education of Young Children)* Young Children. March, 2010. 30-35.

Hannaford, C. (2005). *Smart Moves*. Utah: Great River Press.

Houston, J. (2004). *Jump Time: Shaping Your Future in a World of Radical Change*. London: Sentinent Publications.

Ratey, J. MD. (2013). *Spark: The Revolutionary New Science of Exercise and the Brain*. New York: Little Brown and Company.

Schneider, EF. (1998) SLAM (Speech Language and Movement for Children). Presented for UNESCO Dance International, Stockholm, Sweden.

Schneider, EF. Active Communication Therapy for Children. Presented to Head Start National Conference. 1990.

Understanding Your Child through Brain-Based Research

Aamodt,S. and Wang.S. (2011). *Welcome to Your Child's Brain*. New York:MJF Books.

National Scientific Council on the Developing Child, 2004.

Siegel, DJ. (2010). *Mindsight*. New York: Bantam Press.

Siegel, DJ. (2012). *The Developing Mind*. 2nd edition, New York: Guilford Press.

Tippett, K. (2008). *Speaking of Faith*. New York: Penguin Press.

About Crescendo Publishing

Crescendo Publishing is a boutique-style, concierge VIP publishing company assisting entrepreneurs with writing, publishing, and promoting their books for the purposes of lead-generation and achieving global platform growth, then monetizing it for even more income opportunities.

Check out some of our latest best-selling AuthorPreneurs at http://CrescendoPublishing.com/new-authors/.

About the Instant Insights™ Book Series

The *Instant Insights™ Book Series* is a fact-only, short-read, book series written by EXPERTS in very specialized categories. These high-value, high-quality books can be produced in ONLY 6-8 weeks, from concept to launch, in BOTH PRINT & eBOOK Formats!

This book series is FOR YOU if:

- You are an expert in your niche or area of specialty

- You want to write a book to position yourself as an expert

- You want YOUR OWN book – NOT a chapter in someone else's book

- You want to have a book to give to people when you're speaking at events or simply networking

- You want to have it available quickly

- You don't have the time to invest in writing a 200-page full book

- You don't have a ton of money to invest in the production of a full book – editing, cover design, interior layout, best-seller promotion

- You don't have a ton of time to invest in finding quality contractors for the production of your book – editing, cover design, interior layout, best-seller promotion

For more information on how you can become an *Instant Insights™* author,
visit **www.InstantInsightsBooks.com**

More Books in the
Instant Insight™ Series

CrescendoPublishing.com

Made in the USA
San Bernardino, CA
25 February 2017